The Rants and Ravings Of a Modern Day Cave Dweller

Poetry and Verse

By

Joseph Timmons

This Book is dedicated to:

My Parents, Leroy and Dora Timmons

My Lovely Wife Yekaterina

And to My Children

Michael

Alexander

Gustav

Rita

Vera

Without You, Life would not be Possible

Table of Contents

Poetry, as I write it, an informal introduction

I was born in Brooklyn N.Y., it was 1965; from there it was all downhill, no not seriously, I had a great childhood, I grew up in Long Beach, N.Y. which was a quiet an unassuming town, actually it is a sandbar on the coast, but it was home, and it still is although now I live in California. I grew up during the 70's and 80's and learned about life from shows like "laugh in" and "Scooby doo", not much but it was interesting. It was during picture day at school, here I am, at 5 years old, I can remember exactly what I was thinking at this moment "Is this how things will be forever?", as a child I never thought of growing older, just growing up, I thought life would be as it was. As I got older, I saw that I was very wrong.

I have no impression of myself as having a gift or something of altruistic importance that makes me some sort of literary god, that I think you should be impressed with my work, I just think I have an opinion that matters to me, and I would like to see how many of you feel the same way about life. I like to torment my friends this way, and I think of you as a friend if you read my work and feel any of the feelings I do. My work bounces around like a flea on a sand mound, feverishly looking for something to hold on to.

I first got the idea to write when I was 12, I would read poetry and it would fill me with romantic ideas and thoughts of life as being spiritual and free, then one day while walking home I saw an ambulance in front of the neighbor's house, their grandfather had passed away while eating lunch. They were carrying his body out and I watched as he was lifted in the gurney, the cover fell away and his eyes were open, he looked so sad, like he forgot something, like he was not finished with what he had to do. It was at that moment that I realized that life can be cruel as well as beautiful, and why I must write, to finish what I started.

I believe it is common to consider that poetry must rhyme or be in verse, for me I conceive that poetry is an inner expression and does not have to be "historically" set in specific stance. I would like to present to you some of my views in an introspective way, the world as seen through my eyes and felt through my heart. I would not expect everyone to gain a sense of awe or wonder by my words, but if you take the time to look at the way it is composed, you may find it enlightening. I think too much has been placed on the way that poetry or works of literature should be presented in a certain way. When we stepped out of the darkness and began to communicate, we had to develop from grunts and gestural movement to complex languages. The human race has grown into many cultures with many forms of independent expression; however the desire for beauty and culture has similar traits in all languages. It is through desire to be close to enlightenment that we write our thoughts down, this is the reason that we take the time to express our inner feelings on paper, for the future generations to see our lives truly unfettered.

With this book, you will be able to see what it is like to be someone else, in all of this person's joys and sorrows. People have the uncanny ability to be forgetful and under appreciate the things in their life, I have, and I learned from it... sometimes.

I am however a procrastinator and didn't start sharing my mental depravity with the general public until now. I prefer to think I was waiting for a bus (to get hit by of course) or maybe inspiration, maybe inspiration drives a bus. Anyhow, enjoy my prose, ignore the cons and try not to laugh at me as you pass me by on the highway of life, love and the pursuit of an all-night coffee house on the outskirts of humanity. My wife and I will be there with our 5 children fixing the flat on our minivan. I hope that you do find some joy in being me, even if just for a day. This book is written for just that, living my life, as I have

The Poetry will now Begin….

It's not too late to put this down and run away…………..

OK, I warned you.

For my friends

I’m sorry
For all the things I’ve done
To,
And put you through
I never meant to do it
But
I was on a roll,
I went with it

But, remember
I warned you
How, well…
I said hello
I introduced myself and you failed to escape

Anyway, slap yourself on the wrist
I warned you and you did not heed the notice
And now you are stuck with me and my loyalty
You have none to blame
But yourself
Don’t blame me

In memory of her

I loved her
With all that I had
My heart and soul
Or so I thought
Our breakup
Painful

My period of mourning
Extensive
... I think I am over it now

Years have passed
Many loves since
Now
To go on

I see her face in every window
In every thing
It doesn't hurt
As much
As it used to

Did it have to end?
This way?

All I wanted was a tie

Went to the Mall
All I wanted was a tie
Had a real friendly clerk
I got the 50 cent tour

So many things
Bright
    Shinny
        Things

Bought so much stuff
Some needed
    Some not
        Some ...
            Useless
I must have spent...
Uh,
Never mind
I don't care to remember

Only one thing though
I forgot the tie
I'll go back tomorrow
Ill check my ATM first
And hope it is his day off

Wanted Criminal

I got arrested
For as to what the sate considered a
3rd Degree Misdemeanor

A Dog Violation!
An ex-girlfriend
A dog
Was picked up, un-registered and wanted
Me
The gentleman
Bailed it out
No fine paid
She promised she would
She didn't
She used my ID
They came for me
12 hours in lockdown
Hardened for a $ 10.00 fine

The moral of my story
If your ex-whatever's Dog
Gets picked up
Leave the state

Let the dog FRY!

Two parts, One mind, Three Verses

If I live
Will I die?
Cut off my hand
To spite my thoughts
End rambled speech
Just to keep talking?

If you care...?
About all you do...
When will you stop?
To care about everything
Else?

Where I stand
Will I fall?
My opinions
Form a voice
And I will
Speak my mind
If only to myself...

Be heard

Race to the top

Oh no,
Not another ***one***
Not
Another poem
Inciting
To form some reason
To explain some
Random
Thought…

Are you trying to convey?
Some
“Deep” emotion
That you think holds value to my life
Well
I’ve got something to say
And tell you in short wording

I wrote this first!
Nyeahh!
So There!

Where it all began

I love the smell of coffee in the morning
The “click” of my lighter
The morning’s first smoke
In the bathroom mirror
My eyes hazed and turns away at the sight
Of myself

In the Kitchen
Eggs, become Breakfast
An Homage, to my hunger
Lounging by my window
Soft, sweet Jazz on the box
Interrupting an almost perfect silence

As the haze lifts from my eyes and the day begins
My desk, lit by the sun, my pad calls to me
I say to myself
“Not yet, after the shower”
But yet, the pen looks so lonely, with a tear of ink cresting its tip.

A Warrior’s Haiku

Standing tall
Against the Storm
Deny Oppressions Aim
To Subdue my Spirit and Soul

Clown’s Haiku.... *Bless You*

Pratfall, Curtain Call
Confetti Rain
“Smell my Flower”
Squirt, All Wet

Poet’s Haiku...*Pass the Sugar*

Depressive Boredom
Obsessive Prose
I am Literate, Hear Me Roar...
Oops, Pencil Broke

Back Talk, Double Talk, From One Side

(This poem has in interesting story to it, I was studying for a final exam in my 3rd year of college and my girlfriend at the time was engaging me in a conversation which lead to a breakup of our relationship, and since I was deep in study and basically ignoring her, this is the exact amount of the conversation I remember, verbatim. I, for the life of me cannot remember her side of it. This just proves that men cannot multi-task.)

Yes? (She Knocks on the Door, then enters the room)
No! (She asks if I have time for her)
When, (She makes a romantic offer, to which I cannot recall)
Where, (Reference to a prior conversation)
Me? (Is this my only concern?)
You? (As if she were a distant soul)
Now? (Again, an offer is made)
No? (What was I thinking, I can't recall, was it the square root of 36 or 63)
Wait! (I am trying to gather my thoughts)
Don't! (I see a hand coming my way, flat and open palmed)
Please...? (A request for an end to hostile behavior)
OW! (Request denied)
STOP! (The beating continues)
Halt! (As she hits me in the chest with a Book)
Help! (As her eyes well with tears)
Wait... (I realize I am being released for her heart)
Don't leave (now, I choose now to want to talk)
Me (I am selfish)
Alone (soon to be)
Please... (I beg forgiveness)

I...

Love...

You...

SLAM!

(The door ends it)

RE-HASHED EMOTIONS

In an old Grey sweater
From the 5 and dime
I walked across town
Just to watch the passing scenery
I stopped at a bench to
To rest my legs
Loafing
I gazed at a cloud
And
As it passed me by
I saw
It was doing the same
As me
It began to rain
I thought
"How sad"
Just when both I and the cloud
We're getting comfortable

In the warm drops
I noticed the town clock's time
And realized
That like the cloud
I too
Had to cry
Someday

WHAT MEN THINK PRIVATELY?

Women, pretty neat huh?
Caring
Loving
Look good
Feel good
"Real good"
Only
One thought though
One problem
Getting one
Hoping
They feel
The same
About
You

WHAT TO SAY WHEN YOU ARE THRUST FORWARD SLAMMING HEAD ON INTO THE REALITY OF LIVING IN A MODERN WORLD WITH MODERN RESPONSIBILITIES, LIVING IN OUR TIME

OUCH!
How often the obvious answers elude us all

Embattled

For want of peace
In my mind and body
Empty and hollow
Soul escaping from the cracks
In my skin
My armor
Dented, pitted and rusty
Unarmed
Facing my inner enemies
I let out a muffled cry
My words unheard
Uncared for my passion suppressed
Not by choice, my hands bound
Not by want, I feel nothing
Not even the cold, I fear my mind is lost
For I have nothing left to loose
But it
Old soldier
I have lost this war
This game
I have played well, but ill strategized
The game has beaten me
I succeed, but the game plays on
I am without
A move

SIMPLE LOGIC

As moments pass
Like a grain of sand
Each has its place
It seems
So simple
Until you search deeper
For the meaning's in the picture

Like each grain
No two the same
Only similar in design
Each to make
Hat they may
Like each moment
No matter how small
Are timeless
Unto themselves

"Oh Man
See thyself not superior
Just unique
Only to thine own self be true"
Like that grain
That moment
Your coming
Your passing
That
May be forgotten

It is yours now!
That will survive you… Eternal.

UNTITLED

Stillness
Quiet
The dark
Sandy shore
As sandpipers call
To the gulls
Signaling when crumbs are sighted

When standing in the gates of evolution
Revolution
Cycle complete
From where we came
We visit occasionally
Remembering when
It all began

WHERE IT ALL BEGAN

I love the smell of coffee in the morning
The "click" of my lighter
And the morning's first smoke
My eyes hazed at my sight of myself in the mirror

In the kitchen
Eggs become breakfast
Lounging by my window
Soft Jazz on the box
Interrupting an almost perfect silence
As the haze lifts from my eyes, the day begins
My desk lit by the sun and my pad calls to me
I say to myself
"Not yet, after the shower"
But yet, the pen looks so lonely

But I repeat myself.

NO HOPE

Sterile
Environment
Complacent voices
Docile souls
Weak and broken
Empty minds that weep
Mundane art that is not
Iron fist
No freedom
Eternal hell
Everlasting

Thus the end of civilization
The spark of humanity has gone

Out

I THINK

Sobriety tend to hinder
The positive flow towards
The subtle indifferences of apathy

But I just don't care

WHY WAIT FOR THE END TO COME

Time is irrelevant
Inconsequential to the point at hand
Or to the greater scope of this reality
When the end comes, you'll know
Till then, why bother

Want a beer with that?

There never seems to be enough

Once I had a dream
Of flying ships
Dancing nymphs
Sailing the heavens
Calling to me
Singing
To
Me
I want that dream
Again
So now I lay myself to sleep
To dream the dreams
Of youth

Wild in the grass

In the tall grass
On the plains
Lays the big cat
Stalking, waiting
For it's prey
Hungry and ready to pounce
Breathing, heavy and labored
Has not slept, for days
Has not eaten, for days
Has not seen prey, for days
The game has moved on, to lush green valleys
Yet nobody has told, this great hunter
So it waits, furred skin taunt and close against rib and to bone
So hungry, it knows no other life
It will stay and wait, and die someday unmoved
Starved, yet proud
Jungle hunter

I know

I have loved, in my own way
The only way I know
I know love, in my mind
The only mind I know
I have felt love, in my heart
The only way I can feel
You reject me, in every way
In every way that can hurt me
I stand here alone
As my legs buckle beneath me
I lay here, crying in pain
The only pain, I will now and forever know

Nervous

I apologize
For my state
I have never
Done this
Before
You see I am very anxious
Somewhat tormented
Really
By the fact that
I am
Never really sure
If I am actually insane
Or if
It is just a way to escape
The fact
The truth
That I am
Faulty

Seemingly

Seemingly
The founding fathers
Who brought us here
Neglected to mention
That we should never think
Ourselves so bold
As to tell others
How to be
How to be free
How to be free from oppression
By forcing our ideals
Upon others

NOTHING

When you have nothing
You have nothing to loose
But then the IRS
Won't get anything either
The last laugh is often cruel
But worth the wait

Footprints in the Mud

Walking, walking and walking
Wet and sticky
The earth beneath my feet giving way
My life, drags behind me
Like a homeless persons shopping cart
Head down, not to view
The eyes that are watching me
Waiting to see me fall

Uneven and uneasy
Unsure, the earth beneath my feet
Sliding with every step
Backward, like a dancer stepping out of time
Dancing........into Oblivion
Getting dark outside, cold and wetter

The rain coming down, washes away my memory
I fade from view, soon to be forgotten
Wasted years, trying to find hope
I bend down, running my hands through the muck
Hoping to gleam some chance of redemption
Some chance at a life on fertile soil
To watch my dreams grow strong
And not to wilt away

I trudge on, with pain in tow
Supported only by to love of mine
I hope not to fail them
Or myself, while going towards the river banks
The river banks of torment
Which summon me on?

I find a place that's dry, if only for a while
Until the tide comes in
I look upon my feet, tired and swollen
To wipe the mud form my shoes
Mud of sorrow
That rolls back upon itself in my wake

I look at the distance of where I have been
I see no trace; the mud has resettled and covered my steps
No history of me, no signs that I have been
I look forward to where I must go, with hope glazing my vision
Looking for patches of sanity in which to rest my bones
What will become of me now?

Back into the mud I must go
Until
The next moment of peace
The next moment of delight
Wanting the Mud of my life to dry
And praying the is no quicksand
Beneath

Evermore

A Love Sonnet to my Wife

I look up
Into your eyes
As you lay there watching me
I see a young woman with a fire and thirst
A look of desire that holds me where I am
Wanting more
Giving all that you have
To me

Take my hand and walk with me
To the place in your heart
Deep and pounding
My want for you grows
Every day you wake next to me I know that I am thankful
But, what of you?
Do I give you what you desire?

I tend to you
I attend to your garden
Placing what I have in hope that you desire to see it blossom
My love for you in all ways is what I have come to know and need
I trust in my feelings
I feel the need to be with you and deep inside you and your heart

I raise you up upon the altar of my affections
And I worship you and praise you
I am a fool for what I have done
I have committed myself to slavery, but Slave to you and your passions
Not the worst crime
The worst crime would be to waste you, to let you go unloved

The sweet waters of your pleasure enliven me
Fulfill me and feed me
I live off of you, in a symbiotic relation
Though sometimes you may feel like I am a parasite, draining you of life
That may be, but I cannot resist, you sustain me

I know why I love you..............because I do
And that is all I need to know
I may not be the best man, of the man of your dreams
But know this
You are my fantasy, my dream, my goddess
I see you in my mind, my life and in all things

The center of my soul, is you

I take you, and feel you beneath me, holding me
Sometimes it seems that you push me away, but only to let me fall deeper into you
To drink of you and live again
Your touch makes me gasp
Do I deserve you... do I have the right to be with you?
Yes, yes I say because you are mine
All that I have done before this was to ready me for you

Oh you, so young and innocent
My Lolita, my seductress
You have seduced me by not seducing
By not tricking or deceiving
There was no hunt
And to my prey I have fallen
I wish to devour one who is so sweet

You have live many lifetimes
Yet you are as a precious gem, ever shining
A flower, single in the valley, not to be plucked
But gently deflowered
I would gather up those petals, only to place them back

I wish to proclaim to the world my victory in having you, yet share you with the world
As my singular treasure
A testament to my manhood
Yet
I do not own you; I merely am graced by you

Your heart begins a second beat
One for me
One for another
Which is stronger?
I would accept the weaker of the two, if I must
I was meant to be with you
I don't know if you were meant
To be
With
Me

But I willingly accept the terms of your love
My love has no terms
No expiration
But an eternity of forever wanting

To be
With you
To attend you
To serve you
To be your lord and master
To be chained to your feet

To look up and know paradise
And see heaven in your eyes
Paradise in your soul
To hold you in my arms
Evermore

Failure

Failure
The feeling that you
Have lost, all that you
Have worked for
Gone..............

Have I told you, I am a failure
I have lost all self-respect
Self esteem
Self-worth
Everything

If I have done something to offend you
Then I am truly sorry
If I have done something to initiate
This feeling
That you must turn my insides out
And my heart to dust
Then please, continue
Exact your revenge

Life is nothing
Without
Failure
It gives one a chance to see how much better than you they can be
When you are down and reach to the sky for some glimmer
Of hope and affection
The sun is blotted
And you are left cold and wanting
I am cold

Summer Flowers

Blooming bright
Explosions of color
Summer Flowers
Sweet smell upon the air
Young lovers, embrace
Holding up each and
One another
Youth with aspirations
Trust in the future
With hope
And convictions, budding sprouts of love
With age, comes truth
Knowledge of what is
And what comes of
What could be?
So easy comes the ache
Of life
Sorrows growing
Come
Summer flowers

Hide and seek

In the shadows, my memories lay
Waiting
Many lay there, that I try to remember
The good, are but few
And
Outweighed
By the many
The sad ones move
And creep forward, towards the light
And suck me in, into their game
A game of hide and seek
With my heart
They seek, I hide
But after not too long, they find
A way in
To cause me pain
The good ones stay
In the shade
To afraid
To fight, for me
Cowardly memories all
They sit in the shadow of my self-pity
Yet I pity myself as well

Tone

When the bell breaks
And rings no more
No longer
The tone that sets
The motion
Time is judged
With each stroke
Of the hammer
Upon the dome
Yet
Time stands still
No tone
Is rung
My time has come
The day, is done
Peering through the crack
In the bell's dome
As the hammer
Comes to meet me

JUVENILE CHRONIC

Countless times
I kept my tongue
Only speaking
When need be
I never meant to hurt
Inside

I thought it best
For
The general crowd
That by holding back
My venom's
In check
In place
It would not offend
So unsure
Of myself
Of me

When I was younger
I thought how grand
It would be to grow up
I think now that
That
That
I spoiled my youth
Wasted it all away
I fell into the trap
Of maturity
I want to go out and play again

WHAT WILL I SAY WHEN I'M TOO OLD TO CARE

Bent
Broken
Waiting for the fall
Waiting
For the end
I thought "tomorrow"
Tomorrow is a new day
I never
Ever
Thought it would
Be this way
The way
Of the world
Not mine
Not my way
Not my fault
I'm tired
I want to sleep now
Goodnight

Goodbye

A QUESTION

How long
Can one man
Endure
When
All defenses
Is
Spent
And
All that's left
A hollow shell
That consumes
The nothingness
Within

Oh Joy

In all ways uncommon to my life
I try to find you, but you are absent in the wake of my days
Simple, is my mind
I think of you often, in those hours of the sleepless nights
I must so often endure in a cold bed
I seek warmth in you
You that is not present to me in my time of need

Dark and cloudy horizons loom
Drifting clouds of doubt and frustration linger
When the rain comes I am to melt in sadness and fear
Beneath a sun that is black in spirit
Oh my life
Why have you forsaken me to this, a non-person?
A shell
Empty and void

Joy
Oh joy
When will you come to me?
I want to sing with you
To shout from the mountain and proclaim my happiness in knowing you
But my voice is shallow and muted
The lyrics of you elude me
Pestilence would be something to see
Deep within

Joy
Oh Joy
Come to me
Bring me the peace of ages
Bring me my quiet slumber
Nay, not death I speak of
But the gentle sleep of angelic dreaming
The time when I can be happy
And in delight of my days

I cry sometimes
Sometimes I cry out
Time flies... too fast
I am so slow
Weighted down and burdened
By my own self loathing
Pity me, myself and I
The 3 of us are undone

By our own
Hand

I Wonder

I wonder why
Wonder of all
Wonder when
Wonder how
Wonder of all things
Wonder now
Wonder of woman
Not a wonder man
Wonder of god
Wonder of sorrow
No wonder
Wonderful
Wonder less
I wonder away
Wonder-lust
No wonder in my life
Wonder if I am missed
Wonder if I'll be missed
Wonder if
I wonder

From Out of the Darkness

I look out
Peering to the daylight
From within my own cave
A modern day cave dweller
I stomp my feet, pond my fists
Nothing
Not a sound
Not even
An echo
So hungry
But if I go out
Out of my cave
My safe place
Will the light
Burn me
I have been burned
Before

My Life

-A Love Poem for My Wife, Yekaterina-
Just a bit of fun
Before I go, I would like to entertain you
With a song I know
"As I lay with thee in mind"
"I often leave this world behind"
"And as I dream of finer things"
"A simple touch from you, it seems"
"Is all I need to make my life Complete"
"So My Life, My Wife"
Sing with me, the same love song
Ere I go, to sleep alone
And dream no more

Passion

Oh vast and luxurious
My thoughts of you
Pure are my intentions
With nervous fingers
Touching
With eager lips
Kissing
My forever love
Never have I known
The supple and tender joy
Like I know with you
My heart burns and melts away
As time counts down the moments
Until morning
When once more I will awaken
To the beauty that is you
Of morning come slowly
And let this night continue
Never to end
And if it must end, may it revisit us
Over and over
So I may bathe once more in you kisses
And be sustained by
Passion

Sandman

Come now, do not cry
I will lay you down
And whisper sweet lullabies
In your ear
I will hold you
Close to me, and protect you
From the cold, cruel world
I will embrace you, and love you
For the rest of your days
And give you sweet slumber
In all the many ways
Close your eyes, and go to sleep
And if you wake, in the dark of night
Know in the shadows
I will be watching, waiting for you
In sweet torment, with twisted eyes, smiling

Stillness

Quiet now, listen to
The Stillness
Be at one, all within
With the dark and brooding
Silence of the night
My soul, turning, spinning, twisting
Weeping with the wind
Cold and bitter, now
Depress and suppress the feelings of
Pain, if that is what it is or more than that
I am not sure, how "It" began
But I live it now, my life it is
And I want to be free
Come to me now
And show me there is life in this time I gasp for breath
Show me there is hope
Show me
Love

Love

Held within this chamber a Prisoner
Of my desire, I feel Helpless
I would hold you, Embraced
Course skin of my hands
Runs along the soft, smooth
And silken flesh of you
Memorizing every moment
Trembling at my touch
You make me, burning inside
What I need, is you
Yield to me, embrace me

Touch, that part of me that is longing
When, when will you
Feel my love
My love, feel for me
Love
All I want to do
Is love
You
To be, for you
To be
Forever in your thoughts
The world could be
So far away
Come
Dream with me

Lay me down
Entwined in love's embrace
I long for you
You loved me once
But ...what now?
What has changed?
You, whose dreams
Have gone to sleep

I am Here! Here! Before you... standing
Waving my arms and crying out!
Cannot you hear?
My pleas
You scorn me ...Oh, spite!
My heart has grown
Beating only for you

So distant are your beats, I cannot hear them
Why?

My winter love
I would warm thee
Cold, cold heart
I am flesh, thus flawed
I have made my bed
Must you make me lay there with you?
Only to feel alone
Here, I will be
Waiting Love
Love waiting
To be loved
By you
Come back to me
Though you have never left

Distance

Chained to my pain
Bent, over the rail
Tied to weight
Bearing down
On it
Feeling the sting of the lash on my back
Sorrow of what could be ...now lost?
Fault in my every step
Proud you were, once of me
Proud of me
You yet may be
Mouth open yet no sound flows
Just whimpers
And the crashing sound
Of tears, on the pillow
The few inches between us
Feel
Like a mile

Well met

I would say, please
Stay with me
And walk down
This narrow path
Winding on, through the caverns
With cold winds blowing
Place our steps on unsure footings
But hold tight
My hand, and trust in me
My love knows no reservations
Rich am I
In love for you
Delight in your life's measure
And when the end of this road we reach
Together in heavens glen
The spirits of yore
Will meet us both
In love they say
Well met

My time of wanting

Work, so hard
In the course
Of my life
Once in a while
A great while
I can breath
To rest
So tired
Once, the children have grown
And I have
All that I need
Once, when will it be?
But now
In my time, of wanting
Wanting
Rest
To struggle
No more
To sleep

From inside the hell mouth

In the depths
Down, consumed and devoured
Dark recesses
Swimming in pain
Of all the mind's self-pity's
Harsh corners, jagged and jutting
My thoughts, twisted and swollen
I wander
Crashing
Into the walls, hard and smooth
That suppresses my desires for joy
In the state of despair
Confusion, taking me
And holding me down
Sorrow fills mu lungs
Languishing breaths fill the cavity
In my personal hell, of my own creation
Staring out, from behind its teeth
From inside the hell mouth
Out, into the world, courting thoughts of anger
Wishing.............wishing
For either freedom from this life
Or
The end of my torment

A grand familiar friend

People
Like mice in a maze
Scurry, scurry, scurry
Looking
For that elusive
Crumb of hope
The silver lined
Piece of cheese
Our dream realized
Avoid the passions, baits and traps
The world
That snaps or spines
In twain
To make sense of it all
Seems to be
More than it is worth
Red eyes
Shimmering under
The labs florescent sun
Whiskers twitching
Lunge
At a chance
For freedom
From this maze
While clinging to our tails
Tremble, little mouse
Tremble and dream

Once

Once I was Happy
Not a care
In the world
I could lay still
And dream
The dreams, children have
And seem to waste away
I long for this
Now older
Now responsible
Now, so tired
I dream of that time

Once
When I was young
When I was with
You
How I miss
The days of Juju Beans
And lolly-pops
Of candy corn
And soda pop
Saturdays lasted forever
And Mondays
So far away
Of mother's caresses
And a father's hand
When everything was
Magical

That once
When I was
With you
When my summers were golden
When I could fly
When friends were many
And a kiss
Was as magical
As rain
Please wash away my pain
Like you did once
That once
When I was
With you

Once when I was young

Quotes en Mass

"My life hates me"

"What fool am I, not knowing how foolish I've become, playing a fool, not trying to be foolish"

"I could lie to you, but this is far more interesting"

"To hate is easy, to loath entirely is a lifelong passion, and an art"

"I would introduce you, but I like them"

"Damn these opposable thumbs"

"Free moments cost a lot, when time is money and you don't have much of either"

"That was Random enough"

"I would have a panic attack, but I just don't have the energy for one right now"

"My Depression is my own, but my mother always told me to share with others"

"The fact is my dear, you have no clue as to how absolutely underestimated your unintelligence is spoken of"

"I value my life, for all that I have yet not done"

"I would feel sorry for you, but my dance card is full"

"I have found that as I grow older I have developed a growing distain for all mankind... but I still like you"

"I have a love / hate relationship with myself"

"If I feel anything at all right now, it is that I feel sick"

Soul Soup

First, the water of life
Well-seasoned with time
And experience
Blend in excitement and drama
Try not to add too much tragedy
Stir it up
And
Enjoy

I Wonder

I wonder why
Wonder of all
Wonder when
Wonder how
Wonder of all things
Wonder now
Wonder of woman
Not a wonder man
Wonder of god
Wonder of sorrow
No wonder
Wonderful
Wonder less
I wonder away
Wonder-lust
No wonder in my life
Wonder if I am missed
Wonder if I'll be missed
Wonder if
I wonder

Merriment

Tribute to George Carlin and Kurt Vonnegut

I am happy
To know
You
And saddened as we part
You left too soon

Once, now so long ago

My once, now gone
And now I feel looking back
My once, so wasted
That once
So long ago
When I was with
You

From Out of the Darkness

I look out
Peering to the daylight
From within my own cave
A modern day cave dweller
I stomp my feet, pound my fists
Nothing
Not a sound
Not even
An echo
So hungry
But if I go out
Out of my cave
My safe place
Will the light
Burn me
I have been burned
Before

Passion

Oh vast and luxurious
My thoughts of you
Pure are my intentions
With nervous fingers
Touching, with eager lips
Kissing, my forever love
Never have I known
The supple and tender joy
Like I know with you
My heart burns and melts away
As time counts down the moments
Until morning, when once more I will awaken
To the beauty that is you
Of morning come slowly
And let this night continue
Never to end
And if it must end, may it revisit us
Over and over
So I may bathe once more in you kisses
And be sustained by
Passion

Mine

This is mine
Mine
And mine alone
I own it
I horde it
I obsess over it
The center of my life
All that I have, pale by comparison
It is the one thing
That none can take from me
It will always be
Mine
It is the pain
The sorrow
The misery
Of a broken heart
2 dead halves
Struck
During the beat
Bleeding
Within my chest

When

when
now
always
to be
never
to see and end
and again
and again
so many days
so few hours
so little time
so few moments
yet a lifetime
spent
in search of you
my love
when again
is it time
again
may I see you
again

may I love you
again
and again
and again
and again
if not now
when
when
when

I live my life for you
I live my life with you
I am Obsessed with you
I love you
now, my love now
This is the when
the when is
now

For the young

Life is
For the young
Carefree and full
Of dreams
The young have the means
To make of their lives
All that they desire
Within the blink of an eye
With a glimmer of hope
And trust in the future
But for the me
There is only the truth
The realization
That dreams are for
The young
Not for me
Not for the one
Who has worked all his life
Nothing to show
But empty cups of wonder
Empty beds
Empty dreams
Empty hearts
Dreams are for the young
Who have the time
But time grows shorter
Between each breath
And time can dance the two-step
Upon the heads
Of older dreamers
But keep dreaming
Keep wishing
Keep hoping
Keep trying
Keep
Something

This page was intentionally left blank

Like the stare of astonishment
And wonder
Of why
You bought this book
And why
They let me write it
The End............ Maybe

FINAL WORDS

My poems were not meant to inspire you, or give you some great perspective or light on life. If they have given you some inspiration or have given you pause to search deep within, well… I would believe you to need just as much therapy as I do. I've done my time and I've done my thing, now go do yours. This has been for me one big therapy session, and you my therapists or victims as it may be. If you could, find it in your hearts to forgive me, please. I'll do it again though if you let me, sociopaths tend to do that to their victims frequently.

Draw your conclusions where you may, remember, Mr. Spock said it best, *"In an insane world, it is a sane man who appears insane."* – If this is true, ***if this is true, I am in big trouble.***

Thank you, the check is in the mail.

www.ingramcontent.com/pod-product-compliance
Ingram Content Group UK Ltd.
Pitfield, Milton Keynes, MK11 3LW, UK
UKHW041839200726
13854UKWH00003BA/1219